**This book has been
purchased by BGS Library
for students to use and
enjoy in form rooms.**

Please look after this book and
return it to the book box.

Killer Predators

PAUL HARRISON

W
FRANKLIN WATTS
LONDON • SYDNEY

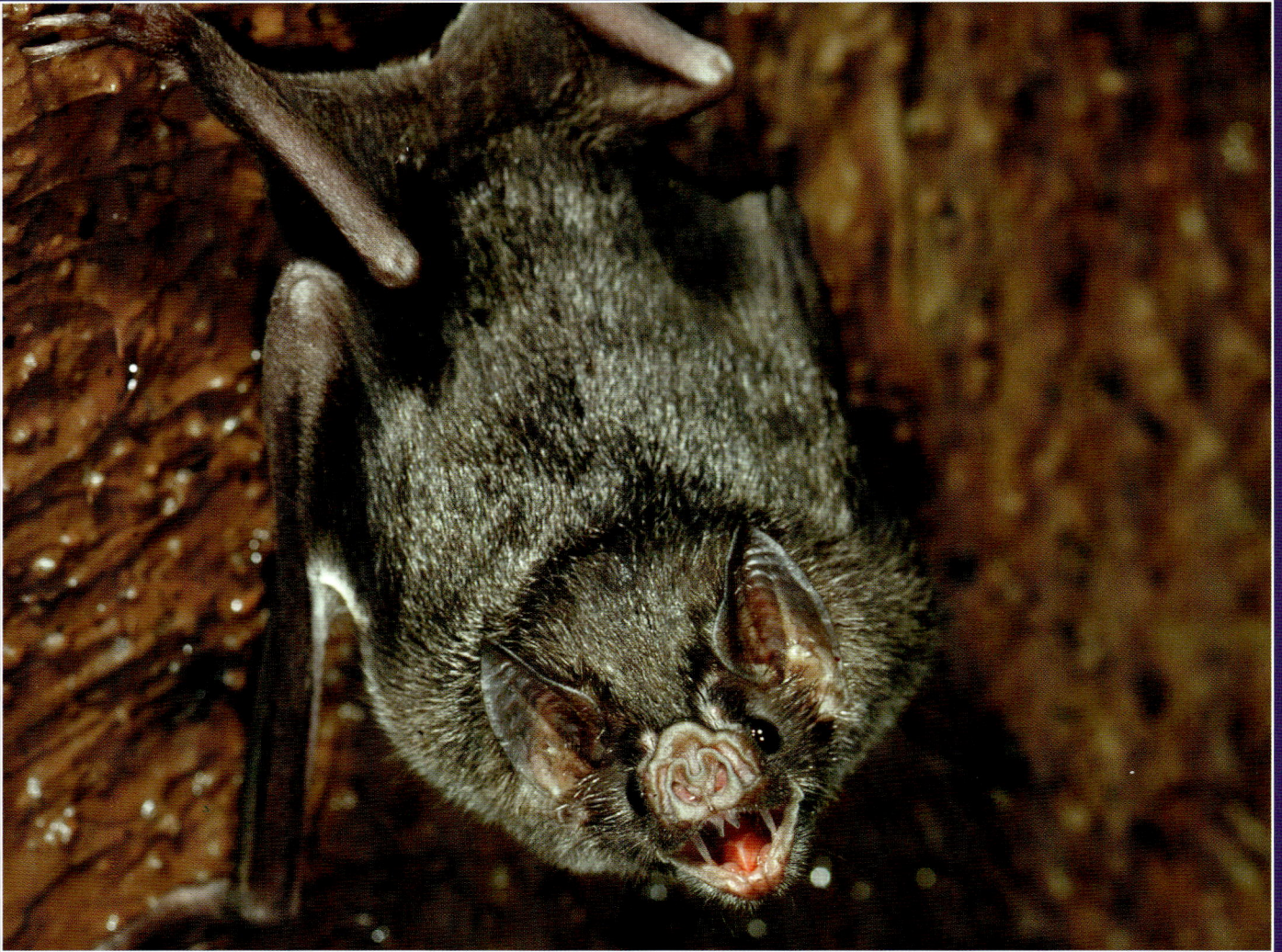

Published in 2009 by Franklin Watts

Copyright © 2009 Arcturus Publishing Limited

Franklin Watts
338 Euston Road
London NW1 3BH

Franklin Watts Australia
Level 17/207 Kent Street
Sydney, NSW 2000

Author: Paul Harrison
Editor (new edition): Fiona Tulloch
Designers (new edition): Trevor Cook, Sally Henry

Picture credits: Nature Picture Library: 4 top, 7 top, 13 top, 18 bottom, 19 top and bottom; NHPA: title page and 7, 2, 4 bottom, 5 top, 6 left and right, 7 bottom, 9 top and bottom, 11 top and bottom, 12 top and bottom, 13 bottom and back cover, 15 top and bottom, 17 top and bottom, 18 top, 21; Science Photo Library: 20 top and bottom; Visuals Unlimited/Corbis 10 top.

A CIP catalogue record for this book is available from the British Library

Dewey number: 591.5'3

ISBN: 978-0-7496-9214-8
SL000957EN

Printed in China

Franklin Watts is a division of Hachette Children's Books, an Hachette UK Company
www.hachette.co.uk

Contents

Meet the Meat Eaters

Predators are the meat eaters of the animal kingdom. They come in all sizes and have lots of different ways to kill prey.

TEAM WORK

When the prey is as quick and strong as elk, buffalo or caribou, the only way to work is as a team. The wolf pack chases the herd until an old, sick or very young animal gets separated. They chase the unfortunate one until it's exhausted, then move in for the kill.

AMBUSH

The crocodile is an expert in sudden attacks. It waits in the water with just its eyes and nostrils showing. When an animal comes along for a drink, the crocodile bursts from the water and grabs it.

HIDE AND SEEK

The ability to blend into the background is a big advantage when stalking your next meal. The bold colours of the tiger allow it to hide easily in the dappled forests and long grasses where it hunts.

BIGGEST KILLER

The most dangerous predators the world has ever seen are living today and they are all around us. We're talking about Homo sapiens, or humans, responsible for wiping out plenty of other species.

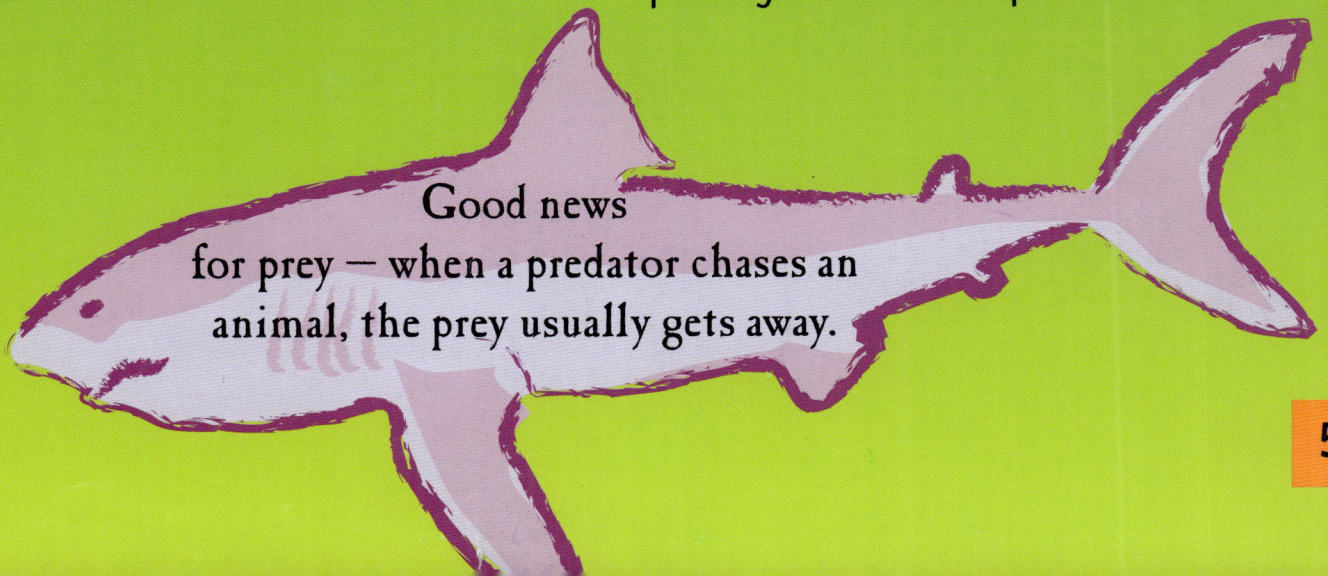

Good news for prey — when a predator chases an animal, the prey usually gets away.

In the Water

70 per cent of the Earth's surface is covered with water and it contains some of the the world's meanest predators.

PREDATORS IN PERIL

The shark is the ideal sea predator. These animals are fast, streamlined and perfectly designed for hunting. The big sharks can tackle pretty much any other fish in the sea.

DEADLY JELLY

Some jellyfish have tentacles 30 metres long, loaded with stinging barbs. A creature straying among the tentacles is injected with poison and pulled into the jellyfish's mouth.

GIANTS OF THE SEAS

The biggest animals of the seas are also the biggest predators. Sperm whales love eating giant squid. Many whales bear the scars left by battles with giant squid.

Orcas, known also as killer whales, have been known to chase seals (their favourite food) right up onto the beach.

FEARSOME FISH

Piranha fish live in shoals and are found mostly in rivers in South America. They have extremely sharp teeth and can eat any animal that comes their way. They rarely attack people – unless they're really hungry!

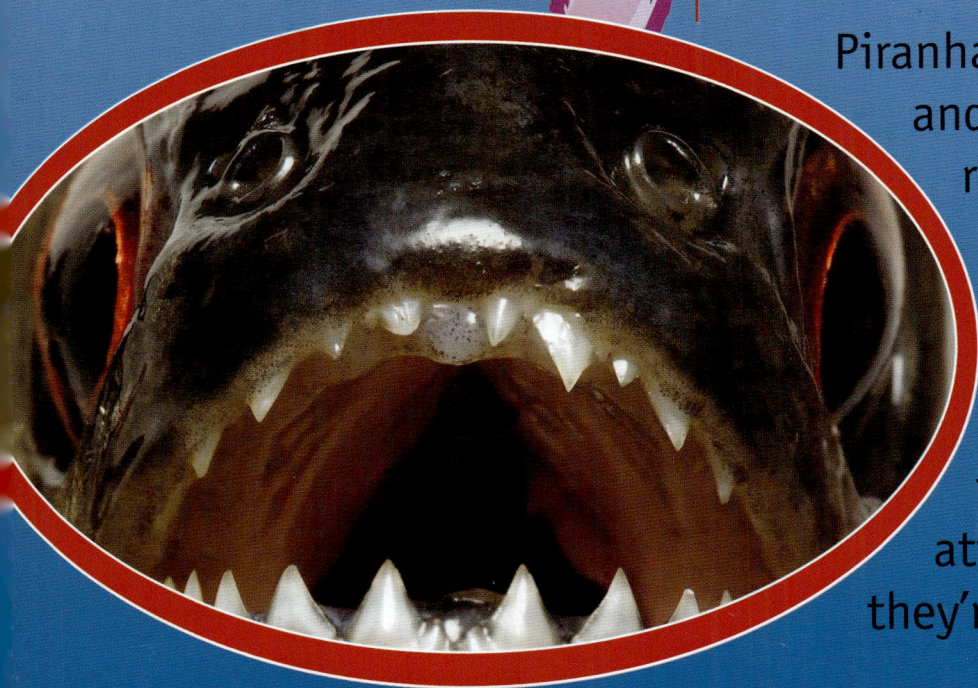

THE HUNTER, HUNTED

Over-fishing, trophy-hunting and the cruel practice of removing fins for shark fin soup, are driving some of these perfect predators to the brink of *extinction*.

The box jellyfish kills more people than all the species of shark put together.

KEEP SMILING

Groupers are fish that aren't built for speed. Their preference is to lie in wait under cover, then grab passing prey and swallow it whole. They have few teeth. Instead, there are thick plates in the back of the throat that can deal with bony fish, octopus, crab and lobster.

Tiny Terrors

The vast majority of the world's killers are from the insect world, and won't harm us at all. But for their prey, they're deadly!

TRAPDOOR TERROR

The trapdoor spider constructs a hole in the ground with a trapdoor on top. It makes tripwires from web and when a passing insect touches one, the spider jumps out and grabs it.

NOT A PRAYER

The praying mantis lies in wait and relies on *camouflage*, and keeping perfectly still to surprise its victim. It gets its name from the pose it adopts while it's waiting for lunch to appear.

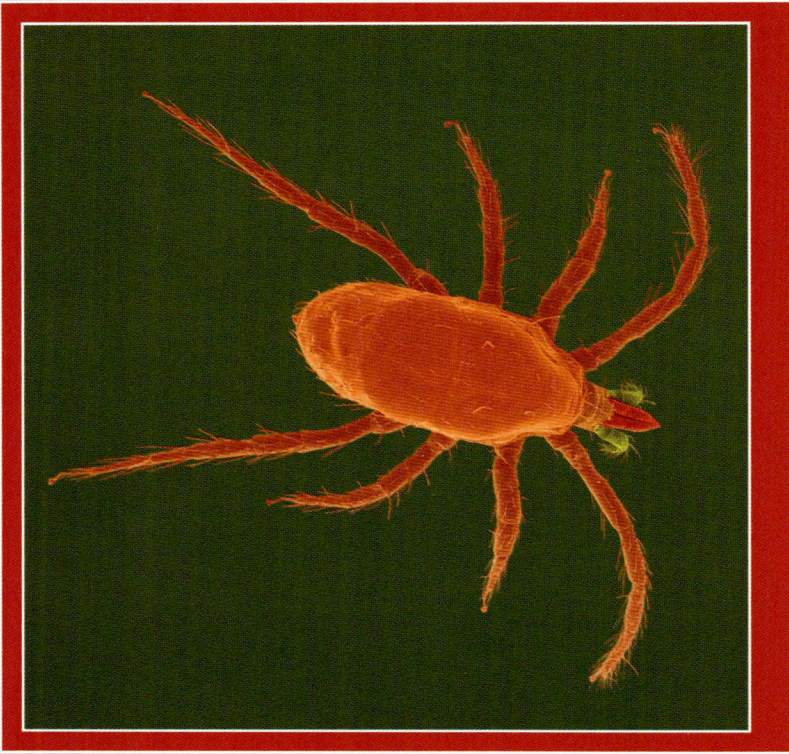

A MITE DANGEROUS

The tiny spider mite is hated by gardeners because it can spread disease and ruin crops. There are several larger and faster mites which prey on smaller mites, helping to control the numbers of spider mites.

GROUND CONTROL

Any garden creature that spends time on the surface of the soil may be prey to the ground beetle. They have powerful jaws and can tackle animals much bigger than themselves.

EATEN ALIVE

Some of the Braconidae family of wasps lay their eggs inside caterpillars. The eggs hatch, then the wasp larvae tunnel out of the caterpillar to build *cocoons* on the victim's skin. If the caterpillar survives all this, it doesn't last much longer!

Some small predators such as the funnel web and black widow spiders have venom powerful enough to kill a person.

HELPFUL KILLERS

Insects that prey on other types of insect can be really helpful – especially to gardeners. Perhaps the most famous is the ladybird which eats aphids and greenfly on plants.

Wings of Death

A nimals spend a lot of time looking out for enemies — alert to the dangers around them on the ground. But what if the threat is from above?

GOING BATTY

Some bats are predators too. Moths and other flying insects need to look out when night falls. Bats use their high-pitched calls as a kind of radar, to find their prey. They judge the position of other flying things by listening to the echoes that come back from them.

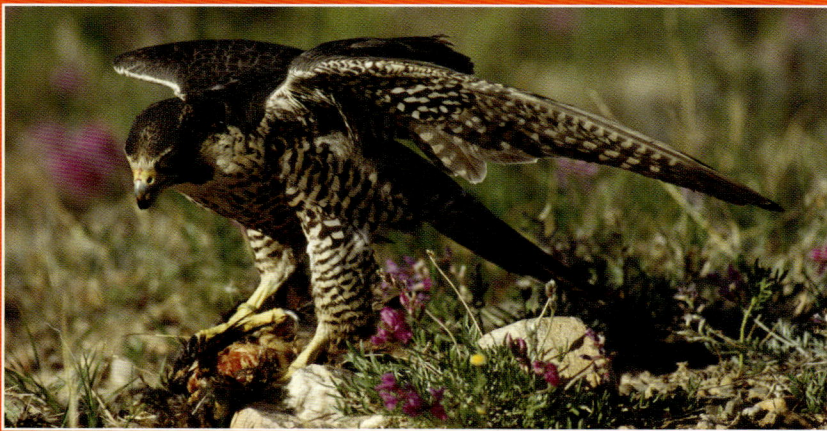

SPEEDY KILLER

The spectacular peregrine falcon focuses on speed. The falcon circles slowly in the sky and spots its prey. It then swoops down and takes its victim in mid-air.

BIG MOUTH

Some birds like nothing better than a hearty fish supper. Pelicans look awkward on land but are good fliers and excellent at fishing. They have a huge pouch under their bills which they use to scoop up small fish.

Fish scales run from front to back so its best to do what the pelican does — swallow them head first!

I CAN SEE YOU

Big eyes with big pupils are a huge advantage to seeing when it gets dark. One kind of bird that relies on excellent eyesight is the owl. It can detect small animals moving around in the gloom, which is great as that's what many owls like to eat.

13

IN AT THE KILL

Despite their fearsome appearance, most vultures are *carrion* feeders. They wait for the animal to die before moving in to feed.

Fish eagles dive into the water talons first, sometimes totally submerging themselves.

SOUNDS LIKE LUNCH

As well as eyesight, many bird predators use their fine sense of hearing to stalk their prey. The Northern harrier, found in Europe and North America, can detect a field mouse by ear at a range of 30 metres.

Cold-Blooded Killers

R eptiles and *amphibians* are cold-blooded. Without the sun to warm their bodies, they can be sluggish. They can still make excellent predators, so beware!

REAL-LIFE DRAGONS

The biggest lizard is the Komodo dragon, a monitor lizard found in Indonesia. Over 3 metres long and weighing over 130 kg, the adult has sharp claws and *serrated* teeth. They can bring down deer or buffalo.

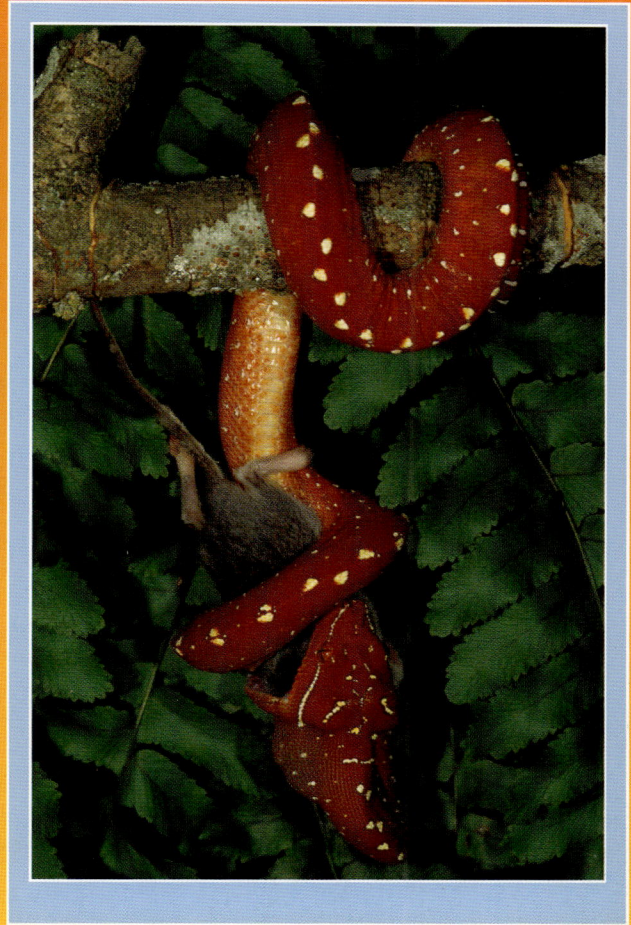

CRUSH ON YOU

All snakes are predators but they use one of two hunting methods. Constrictors, like pythons, crush their prey, then often swallow it whole! The python can unhinge its jaw so it can swallow its meal without chewing.

15

SPEEDY IGUANA

The fastest land reptile is said to be the spiny-tailed iguana of Costa Rica. It has been known to travel at speeds of up to 33 kilometres per hour.

JELLYFISH BEWARE

The leatherback turtle is found in tropical waters around the world. It is a major predator on jellyfish. Jellyfish feed on fish *larvae* and reduce fish numbers. Having this turtle around is good for the fish, and good for fishermen.

FANG-TASTIC

An effective way that snakes use to kill their prey is by biting and injecting their victim with poison. The poison runs from special *sacs* above the teeth, along grooved or hollow teeth into the body of the prey.

The largest poisonous snake is the king cobra which grows to over 4 metres long.

NOW YOU SEE IT...

The chameleon's famous for its ability to change colour to blend in with the background. It's also able to remain motionless for long periods of time, and then suddenly shoot out its tongue and catch insects.

17

Teeth and Claws

Bears, cats, humans and whales are all *mammals* — and we're all great predators!

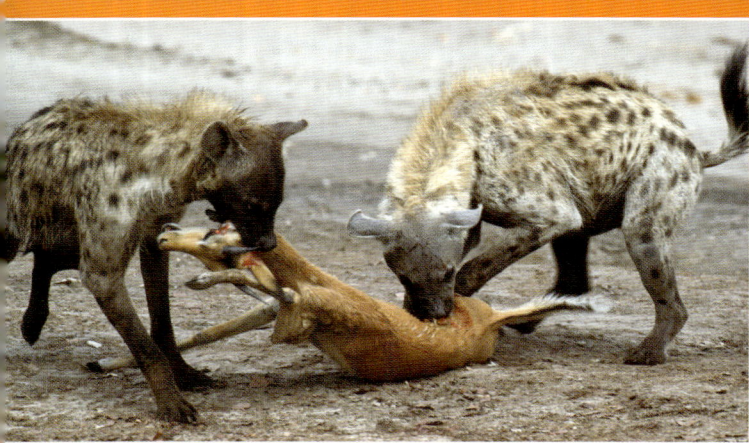

BONE CRUSHERS

Hyenas are known as *scavengers*, but they're very good hunters. They're aggressive, intelligent and work as a team. They have jaws strong enough to deal with bones and hooves, but their size puts them below lions in the predator league.

SEAL SURPRISE

The polar bear's favourite food is seal. It waits around breathing holes for the seal to surface, then scoops it out of the water with a sweep of its mighty paw.

ON THE RUN

Many mammal predators are small, such as foxes, weasels and moles. One of the most aggresive is the American mink. It eats birds, fish, insects, even other small mammals. Unfortunately for the mink, its fur is attractive to humans. Minks are now often farmed rather than trapped in the wild. When a mink sometimes escapes, it's bad news for the local wildlife.

A pack of hyenas is called a clan.

SPEED MERCHANT

The cheetah is the fastest animal on land. It can reach speeds of around 100 kilometres per hour. It can only do this in short bursts of around 20 seconds; so if the animal it's chasing can avoid capture for that long, it might be safe.

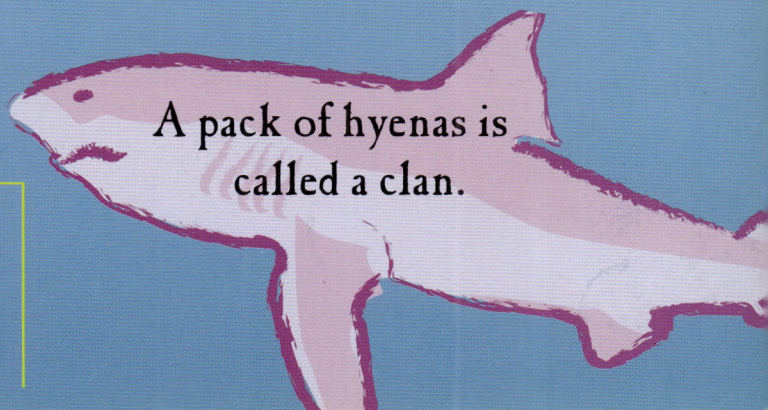

19

Ancient Terrors

I mpressive as they are, the meat eaters of today would be no match for some of the carnivores of the past. Here are a few of them.

MEGA SHARK

Megalodon was a formidable predator. It cruised the oceans until 1.5 million years ago. It was twice the size of a great white shark – it could have eaten it for breakfast!

TEAM TACTICS

Ferocious claws and teamwork enabled the lightweight *Deinonychus* to take on prey much bigger than itself – and win.

TERROR BIRD

The sharp beak and claws of the ancient *Phorusrhacos* tell us that it was a predator capable of ripping and tearing at its prey. At 2.5 metres in height, it was as big as a modern ostrich. Some scientists believe it was alive late enough for humans to have seen it!

THE BEAR FACTS

The fate of the short-faced bear, which died out around 11,000 years ago, is something of a mystery. It was half as big again as any modern bear. Some scientists think it was just too big to hunt easily.

Some people believe that megalodon is still alive today — not that anyone has seen one!

21

Glossary

Amphibian
Animal that can live on both land and water

Camouflage
A pattern designed to make it hard to see something against a background

Carrion
The flesh of dead animals

Cocoon
Kind of cover that young moths and other insects make to protect them while they are growing

Extinction
Reduction of numbers to the point that an entire population dies out

Larvae
Worm-like young insect that has left the egg but has yet to change to adult form

Mammal
Kind of animal that feeds milk to its young

Predator
Animal that catches, kills and eats other animals

Reptile
Animal whose blood is changed by the temperature around it, and that usually lays eggs

Sac
Bag-shaped part of plant or animal

Scavenger
An animal that feeds on carrion instead of hunting its own prey

Serrated
With a sharp edge like a row of connected teeth

Further Reading

Predators
J H Haynes (Top Trumps series), 2007

Octopus and Squid
Mary Jo Rhodes, Children's Press
(Undersea Encounters series), 2006

Raptor! A Kid's Guide to Birds of Prey
Christyna Lauback, Rene Lauback and
Charles W G Smith, Storey Publishing,
2002

Fierce Predators
Ticktock Media (Clever Clogs series),
2006

Deadly Reptiles
Andrew Solway, Heinemann Library,
(Wild Predators series), 2005

Scorpions
William John Ripple, Pebble Books,
2002

Sharks and Whales
Dorling Kindersley, (Ultimate Sticker
Books series), 2004

Index